TREADING WATER, ICEBERGS

***Treading Water, Icebergs,* a mythopoetic** self-creation story that takes place in the speaker's childhood, a psychiatric hospital, and the family's Illinois farm, burnt by fire, takes the reader on a journey of perception—hers, others, and that of her father, his memory compromised by Alzheimer's. Resounding with the thrills of lyric experimentation ("sight-glaciers," a "final gelid slit") as well as narrative reportage from the scenes of a destabilized reality, this emergent voice—determined to float or swim, and not drown—delights in the fractures of meaning and sense, and of identity and representation, with a poet's confidence in making sounds and images, at last, cohere. A "reincarnation adventure" of the highest order, Goold shows the reader "how to distinguish where worlds meet," with a deft musicality and earthly, sensory exactitude recalling Niedecker, Bishop, and Plath. Whether planting bulbs, caregiving, questioning consciousness and systems, or painting rain, this is a new pastoral with able footing both in late modern and postmodern idioms ("you don't need/ metaphor to see the animal that you are"), one that delivers what it promises: to endure, love, and abide.

Virginia Konchan

Annie Goold's *Treading Water, Icebergs* shows empathic tension in its textures, tangles, and clusters. With an intense bravery, Goold treads caring for an aging father, mental illness, suicidality, and the transformation of the self. These poems' dense, knotty language effortlessly splices clarity with invention. This is a book about using poetry for psychological resoluteness. Her language is the native tongue of her alone.

Sean Singer

Treading Water, Icebergs

Annie Goold

SPUYTEN DUYVIL
New York City

ISBN 978-1-956005-53-0

Library of Congress Cataloging-in-Publication Data

Names: Goold, Annie, 1989- author.
Title: Treading water, icebergs / Annie Goold.
Description: New York City : Spuyten Duyvil, [2022] |
Identifiers: LCCN 2022003574 | ISBN 9781956005530 (paperback)
Subjects: LCGFT: Poetry.
Classification: LCC PS3607.O59246 T74 2022 | DDC 811/.6--dc23/eng/20220215
LC record available at https://lccn.loc.gov/2022003574

Treading Water, Icebergs

CONTENTS

My Animal of Then

A man I like to listen to

is laughing, giving me a handhold
beyond my steering wheel:

wintered, the hills float back
on the blue-dust of branches, hemming

this hose of road so abruptly traversable.
Were it not for dog snores

turning my face from front, I'd believe
the world a thing distant to now,

the split sight-glaciers sprinting to my lee.
To see you now, friend,

I apologize for my animal
of then. How do you enter

a pool? Do you mind if you're seen?
I used to, mind that is.

Now it's about the water and not
making a move unearned. I wait

for the waves I make to smooth back before
dipping down further. Any breath held under

soon shatters for breath above, so I tend to leave
my mouth for last. Are you at home

in the city, the one we considered
on night ceilings, cars and cars away? It was for me.

Deer in bloat by the median; another
protracted groan and repositioning, another

titter at his own joke. I should get back
to what I'm doing. I've got parents to see.

ADVENT

i. advent

A broken egg of apricot nectar mottling mauve
cirrus, rousing a flush to the preposterous ledges of winter
dunes: achromatic wind runnels—the same that turvied
with ferality the fallow corn stalks and bean reeds the night prior
—pacified, wading the up. Gabardine sward; thousands of spent
matchsticks peeping between calcium hares; parallel, ditches

let shard their ice caps, breaking their bridges to the regiments.
Taking a turn to the east, the trenchant grain elevator amuses
its solo spoke self with the complementary palette before being done
with day's light, trying out its foxhole green epidermis with orpiment,
copper beech, sumac, tungsten. Thoughtful hedonist. Second
passenger, a humor, lances itself, proceeding with the deepening

wheel ruts, their minced lime stones gesticulating preferred conduct.
Maybe it's due procedure, this companion letting. That which gathers
can pour. Decisively not an omen: the road's only slick at the mouths
of the driveways. Mark the bare dogwood and as high holly,
slipping to profile silhouettes in their jockey for the front door:
the egg has clotted in a house-shaped shuck.

ii. from the kitchen bay window, '06

Rose hip magistrate, high as his pin
oak's ambition: our gentleman cardinal is not having it,
this frozen sand bath, his fin head whet to edge his brood.
The Passer bulbs are game for a final gelid silt
to gloss the wings,
frenzying the yucca's resugared bed; that mud freckled
ubiquity jettisons in glib, revelrous business, a'switch
to switch like loosed arrows. Hoar slipped, the desert
fronds half ring the berrybird, but granular
sweeps mean purpose anew, so the latter faction yields,
knownbound, ruth hexed, sintering.

iii. the basement, '17

Given the vanitas deluge, it's fair to think someone asked
"How long can you tread water?"
while conjoining such matrixes.   Poor someone.

   Yes, there was purpose initially
causing the terracotta toad to vomit stray AAs next to a five-pack of screws
on the PC desk, and the trio of table lamps were disrobed with
clairvoyant reason beside the rimpled, cracker-strong duck
bibs and half-eaten handful of d-Con behind a trophy for corn.
They're of later's means,   the moments when
          stars allow

   time and energy
  to work together in Better Living.

      perennial becoming
  so
there's a river across the laundry room floor where the rain gets in
  so
the treadmill doesn't work
  so
our windsock red bird is ready to collect a breeze
  so
why not store wine and beer on the spare primers
  so
keep on keeping change and tractor bolts in the same coffee cans
  so
shall the cardboard fruit crates maintain their Jenga game on the
          dedrawered dresser
  so
eventual is hope, or maybe the other way around

so

three kids and two full-time, plurally employed parents acclimate themselves

so

as to reclaim rooms when the kids aren't coming back, and you've worked

so

hard to know when it got out of hand, and it's

so

wrung of dignity, being unable to climb up or down a set of stairs

so

you have to stay still if you're going to heal, and I mean have someone else cook

so

it's in the crawlspace, because I can smell it

so

when will it be the time if now isn't it

so

the sunned-to-teals pheasant print stays unhung,
and the anatomically correct rainbow
salmon mobile hurts no one drifting with daddy
longlegs gone to tumbleweed in the corner.
                    Until a shift from the rooms above,
            dum vivimus vivamus.
            I'm not here to fight.

THE DOWNY

Whether he left or stayed, he wouldn't know.
Hitched to stitch a tree as bald as himself,
slipping seedling holes in branches to help
make a store in winter, the black and snow
check his eyes with an afternoon glaze. He goes
and goes and goes back until slack, engulfed
by his own map like some despotic elf.
Urgent, creamy tales of where the gold's sown,
the watch gets (and stays) old. Scrubbing fat tears,
He knots the same story: "Glorious sun,
The sky!" Whacked out sad man and me. Feathered,
fluttering, foul: sheets ice the copse, and it blears
like his blistered red dome. Eager, not done,
he tries again. Up and at 'em. Fuck the weather.

ICEBERGS

1.
As a self
-soothing tic,
my father picks
at the chalky plaque
on his elbows, knees, head.
I drove my mother and father up
-state to a Japanese garden. It took four full
hours to get to a hotel in the city.
My father prefers the front seat
now that he's demoted
to passenger only. I'd started to hear
tick tick tick tick tick tick tick tick tick tick tick tick tick tick tick tick tick tick
early in the trip, thinking it was the windshield wipers.
I looked down: a pile
an actual pile
on the crotch of my father's pants
had accumulated. I couldn't
see his right elbow, but from the spots
I'd seen in his sheets and on his pillows,
and on his sleeves and through his jeans,
I knew he was bleeding, staring at the sky
the whole way. His
favorite phrase, *We clever little chimpanzees,*
gets spread through the days, leaving
a larger and larger trail across each. He moves his hand
to scratch his pink head:
a prairie boy's sky, his eyes.

2.
He's also often saying *Am I tripping?!*
while watching through noon light
the cardinals playing nice with the doves and sparrows at the feeders,
the jays bullying the doves and sparrows away from the feeders,
and the robins just hoppin' ambivalently in the grass.
It's, like, WOW!: We get to live on this gorgeous planet! as a muffin
disappears despite the two-months' old new tremors. Is it time
for the day's garden walk? Ope.
Almost.

3.

On the drive to the garden, I was passing a semi
when one of its rear tires blew, sending a giant tread
directly in front of my Mom's car's front right tire.
I let my parents have their reactions while I simply watched
the tread slide out of sight below the hood.
I pulled off at the next exit. We checked the car over:
a smack of rubber below the light but nothing else.
I went to the bathroom, took a swig of root beer,
and we carried on with the trip north.

4.
Sometimes growing up, I imagined
a rabbit on the wall beside my bed.
It was always a shadow rabbit, a hand idea,
and I narrated in my head its journey
in order to fall asleep.
I never turned off my lamp.

DREAMS AGAIN

I drove my new car into another, a red four door, and ran
not about to get caught. Then, I was
in a bustling, before-times college commons,
froth upon froth of humans brewing in that youth
of frisbees and loosed communal dogs. One young man left
his mouth open yet curled it in a smile at the corners.
He screeched one long owl note forever
and he followed me with his eyes as I passed him,
not acknowledging him or looking for reasons
for his behavior. I woke with acid in my throat.

-

I was in a circle of twenty-somethings, all women,
work friends I'd not made from my undergrad job.
We were balancing in parallel pairs on the lips
of a backhoe's front bucket, assigned to pass
solid aluminum beams back and forth
without falling. I dropped
from the exercise, and I lost
my cool, crying out a weeping,
"I can't take this anymore!
I'm sorry. I'm so, so sorry," not
knowing what for.

-

I'd brought my partner home, and a storm was coming,
that deep prairie rumble and night cloud kicking up
leaves and limbs in sudden cold. I begged to go
to the basement, but we didn't make it. Yet the storm

never hit. It simply became night, the house without
the knocking of consciousness and night-me in the windows.

-

I was in my old dining room, the one my Dad painted
blue one day while my Mom was out. From the doorway,
I saw something leap too high too easily onto a sudden shelf.
It couldn't define itself in shadow, but I knew it
was neither lizard nor insect but something of both.
Then, my mother desperately
hugged me, grateful the creature didn't get me.
She showed me the shredded, four-foot window
screen where it got into the house. Whatever it was,
it was angry and intent.
On the floor, there were these mud-like clods
in patchy trails like shed dog hair.
A bloody flash and my father's arm, gnawed
in his sleep. *There are necrotic spots, Dad*
my older brother said as my father denied pain
and worry. Tunneled into a hood of skin,
his arm ribbeted, and my father smiled.

-

The creature was back, but this time,
the floor was covered in clods.
I looked for my dog, Eleanor, recognizing
this was a murder scene. And she was
fine, just like when she killed that city
rat. Not a bite or scratch. She was still finishing
swallowing the thing, its legs spouting
from her maw like a calf's birth in reverse.
I grabbed the vacuum and watched the clods

through the plastic window spinning inside
the grey detritus in the sucking cylinder.

\-

This time, I was awake, rehashing visiting
the lawyer during the day. The size of Dad
and his tremors struck again, the edges between
his emotional landscape's enormous plateaus,
the red, wind-rounded valleys all shook
from the minutest of capillaries. Again,
the sureness of not having Alzheimer's
has him demanding a second opinion,
some authority beyond all these damn women
softly patting his knee. A man
he can believe, but even when I once more
told him I can protect myself, he said I don't
think you can. *Now, G----, don't forget…*
An absent sugar cone of lemon custard.

\-

I found myself in a tiled world.
I would say mosaic, but really more a porcelain pixel
indoor universe, all in shaded grey and blue.
It turned into the sea, and I floated to the surface
without chop or clarity. The water turned
green and I saw a tiger shark just below my drift.
Like the Lady of the Lake summoned by sword and prayer,
I sprang softly, purely from the water, glittering my way
to an 19th c. ballroom atop the deck of a cargo ship.
The lights in the hall were out, but it being glass
and unstoppably wending stairways throughout,
I was able to evade capture from a demon bug man

out to kill. He transformed into an enormous albino snake
and knit himself through passages, his body both ahead
and behind, making it possible to trick his eye.
In a bedroom, I found a companion and three others
lit from below, and one said *I want to change, to be more*
and his face spread a violet sparkle mask inside his skin,
burbled out two gold fawn horns from his forehead, and we four
leapt away, mortified as he roiled
to a burst as we escaped the room.

—

An infinite chain link fence—the one
I'd run around twice to complete
a cross-country race—and a summer heat.
A burning world overexposed but unacknowledged
for it. There were patrons, but was I
running for them or from them?
The Sun ate us whole.

—

Pigs!

RABBIT, RABBIT

Brave as a child, I carved my initials in the clay.
Ownership didn't have reason to hide then.
As if to prove the act benign, I chose a bunny,
its fur a toothpick-hashed outline, ears baby butter knives,
one bent left and the right straight on.
I even managed a teensy fold to the nose
as it flared in wait. Whiskers akimbo,
knowing such ticklers don't stay the path
by my having the power of privilege enough to raise
a live one at the time. The supreme
strike, though, the eyes. Crudely spooned out
with my puny spike, I'd aimed for the anatomical
placement with eggy hollows, paying
credence to the shape of a true skull. My effort,
a pussycat pink plate mounted with hot
glue to burlap and spare cardboard cut to fit
a square gold frame. Little monkey me
left the funny loom under my art
things in a drawer on the porch, found by Mother
while fishing out ants tunneled in the wood.

MOMMY

Though not a fan favorite, Dad's yellow begonias
find their way into the house as a means into May.
I mowed the lawn while you were gone, just trying
to ease the sequences of the week. Call the painters,
the electricians, the traders of movement and location
for meals and being's maintenance, and I want
so much more for you in a day, each one's fencing hopefully
looser and easier to duck under. The big slow boy
can't move, but you can, and I can, and I dug up a tree.
Several trees, actually, so I know how to break a burrow
in both directions, up and down. We've let the wood
chips in the dying wagon sweeten to a peat, and you've made a path
to and from the backyards' gardens with them, no longer simply letting
mud cake our feet to then scrape off on the door mat with a trowel.
His every morning starting at 1 pm to a subpar cinnamon roll
zapped to life in the microwave and dog pills
hidden in greasy, moldable treats. *It's quiet over here* as we chat, but
he slept through chainsaws above his bedroom one day, so
let's put a record on, the one that you rocked
us to when colicky and wholly resistant to sleep. He has his books,
though he can only restart them, his memory shot to all hell with plaque,
but maybe that's okay. You don't have to rock him to sleep
but to wake him now, and dream cream has brought him a kind
of softness waking life saps, so leave him to it. You're not being
irresponsible leaving him for the market for coffee with me.
You're not doing it wrong. I promise.

Walking, lightened by a green lifting, the deer child flings herself at a false loving, a sensed Adam who holds a ham sandwich and her car keys. She repeats *"The Panic at Needle Park!"*, trying to say *I think I'm like her in her mess of flicking snakes and required shoe rituals.* The Adam heard *I panic at needles* as two witch-angels soothed *We're coming. You're nearly ready, little one. Just hold on.* And the woman on the phone says *No, my name is Pam* and that the deer child should go to the emergency room. Surging to purify herself for repopulating efforts with her sudden Adam, she draws a bath of six tepid cups, because water, it's running out. The world is drying, drying and the road road giggles gurgles in her hands, passing over her forehead, her hair, her hair, her air; the road is a yes, a future of orange sand and children and vexy sexy hexin' lessness at the behest of the crestfall-en gods of all these ivory halls, these paper pants and electric socks, with a teensy red cross and me in a tube where I have to stay still can you do that for me atta girl and we're done

ON UNIT

I have to warn you, our residents are more symptomatic than usual.
We're undergoing construction, too, and that's likely not helping either.

> (I don't know what that means,
> but my [doctor] brother does, so I'll trust them
> but remember that exchange until I understand later.)

Touching other residents on the unit is not allowed.

> (Then why did he pet my leg?
> Or, she grasp my arm like she was about to fall off the earth?
> Why won't that woman stop staring at me and then scurrying away
> talking about me? I just want to sleep.)

You'reagraduatestudentintheEnglishdepartment?!YoucancallmeL.
Tellme:ifAmericancultureismadeupofstolenculturesfromeverywher-
eelse,thenistheresuchathingasAmericanculture?You'refromtheMid-
west,aren'tyou?Myroommatewasfromthere.Shewasreallysweet,butwhite-
girls,y'know?Andshestartedstealingthingsfromme.Youhavetohustlehere.
Theydon'tknowhowtotreatpeoplewhoaren'twhitelikepeople.

(   )

Oh,yeah.Youknowthisisprison,right?

                                                                                    ()

You don't belong here.

                                                                                    ([ ])

31

Jesus Christ! It sounds like the fall of Saigon.

(Mom, am I in prison?)

I'm not sure if you're cleared for this activity. Let's get your weight. Okay. Looks like you'll have to sit this one out.

(oh. But
I didn't mean to. I didn't realize I)

She said she thought you looked like a helpless baby bird.

()

Imeanshecriesalotbutshe'sniceIguessWhenareyougonnacomepickmeup?

(   )

We're working as fast as we can to get you out of here.

(okay.)

The reason why you're here is because you have Bipolar I Disorder with Psychotic Features.

But, it only happened once.

It only has to happen once.

Oh

o

([ ])

but I don't want to be Bipolar.

I know.

June 20th
Sometime in the afternoon I was given a composition notebook

Attempt #1:
I once had a (very fun) day (when I believed I was) of reincarnation while still in the same body. What fears of death, loneliness, continual taking without intending to take, fears of friends and family worrying heedlessly about what would chase me next, were gone.
On that day, I let a horse (in me; by the vet school) out, and I collected three (of my dead grandmother's) four-leaf clovers while galloping onto campus. Earlier, my dog needed a walk (so I let her run off-leash, and she's a dog that doesn't come back when first [or second or third or fourth...] called) and I put her in my car (without her seat belt and harness attached) to take her to (somewhere; likely the off-leash dog park or a national forest I wanted to see or a hiking trail or) a fun place. Sadly, I smelled oil burning (from accelerating too quickly in my blue-green car [that I named Claudia Jean Car {after my favorite character from a beloved show || called West Wing ~written by Aaron Sorkin =while he was ripped on cocaine=~||}]), so I slowed down and parked my car on the side of the road (so I could get [my dog, Eleanor] out before the car exploded [cinematically {painting me a hero ||and a fool|||}]). She was happy to be out of the car (and that made me happy; earlier in the day, there was a car crash outside, very near my new [much more affordable {rat-free ||unmoist|||}] apartment, and I heard the smash, and I'm someone who is a helper, and Fred Rogers said, "In emergencies"—which is what car crashes are—, "look for the helpers. There are always helpers," so I looked for helpers and hurt [beyond my own wounding], and I found both. But I wanted to be [seen as] a helper [in this {and every emergency I will encounter}],

***Went for a walk with V [Staff member {on Behavioral Health Unit}; very kind and patient with me and all peers; got me to realize I could have a fun time while on the unit]

34

Attempt #2:
As I was saying

July 7th
3:12 pm

Attempt #3:
so I helped guide traffic. The elder of two firefighters on scene told me
to get back, so I stepped back and cried/beamed on a wooden fence as
cars wove slowly around the site.) and sprinted loose as a deer, bounding
downhill. I sang and felt the lifecycles of human existence ripple in and
out inside me, as if I was a knowing globe of time projecting its sprawl
in every direction. I wept as I saw old haunts of me and my first rapist/
boyfriend in gratitude for the first time, for a blink of seconds, thanking
what I thought was seeing greater, touching reason, god-like. I heard the
day before (which was still the day I was experiencing [because I hadn't
slept the night prior {and had hardly slept the week prior, tangling in my
sheets, sifting through my head in preparation for a huge, month-long,
cross-country road trip to see my brothers ||and semi-legally acquire lots
of weed||}]), replaying phrases from my therapist and psychiatric nurse
practitioner (thinking they were goddesses and witches [thinking they
were calling to me through time and their eyes and spells I was still too
young to cast yet]), looking for why they were looking at me the way they
did. I had washed my tent in my bathtub and by hand, ridding it of mold
(specifically whatever mold and mildew I'd acquired from the multiple
floods it had survived [leaving the tent damp and never opened]), and
I had to clean it inside (and it took all day, scrubbing on my hands and
knees [while *GIRLS* played {and I occasionally looked up to watch the
show ||I thought I'd loathe ~attempting again~ but really enjoyed and
understood on new, exciting, suddenly appreciative levels||} on my lap-
top]) because it was so windy out, the windiest I'd seen since moving in
(not even one month earlier [praying my security deposit and agreed upon
compensation money would be returned to me before July {which wasn't
and is now a legal matter I have to pursue ||and should have pursued
much, much sooner||}]], but the intoxicant green of the blowing trees

35

Attempt #4:

. I was scared about my trip, too. I didn't want to become Emile Hirsch (playing Christopher McCandless) in *Into the Wild*; I didn't want to be another heavily educated person with a loner complex too severe to know when to ask for help; I didn't want to die by accident of my own ignorance(s) or by whatever this voice inside me saying I am worth killing alone in a forest. I kept wondering how to survive my past (forgetting I already did) and if I'd ever find my person/partner while being the mess that I am. I kept remembering the corncrib where he last raped me, how gorgeous that place is to me, somehow. I asked what do you do when something painful happens somewhere beautiful? Why do these memories keep happening, and why can I remember them too well like this?

(At some point, one morning, while letting Eleanor out, I ran at full speed with her in my tractionless slippers as she chased a thing into grasses. I fell, slid, and whammed the back of my head and scrapped my spine. I told myself, "Don't fall asleep. You're alone. You can't fall asleep.")

Attempt #5:

After I was satisfied with petting the neighbor's dogs rather than direct traffic, I wondered/wandered over to my other neighbors' house, walking straight up to the woman of the house to sit and talk with her on her porch as her dog, Simon, barkedbarkedbarkedbarkedbarked at me until he let me scritchy-scratch him as he was so deliberate in asking. My neighbor asked me how I was doing (having recognized from my red eyes the tears I had already forgotten loosing), and we talked, and I told her I was proud of her for getting out of the former horrors in childhood she escaped. She gave me a cup of coffee as I marveled at the inside of her home, a lived-in space with a live radio scanner, two screens (one a live feed of a security camera pointed in the direction of my apartment's windows, the other playing a Sirius radio station of classic rock music), and tons of family photos, some of which were of military persons, one of whom is serving as a Reaper pilot for the Navy. The coffee had French vanilla creamer in it. It was manna. I said I'd be right back because my dog was barking, seeing me playing with Simon, and I wanted her to be happy instead like I was (and a witch told me she was my daughter [whom I'd mutilated by giving her a hysterectomy as a baby]).

Attempt #6:

I walked back toward my car (after letting E off leash) and saw a horse, a white, flea-flecked horse, standing in what pitiful shade was available in its miserable, chain link pen. Knowing there was someone watching (a camera? a goddess? a miniature backhoe.), I shrugged a quick, "Sorry," and let the enormous runner out (believing it was another family member, and I patted its side as I told it while tapping my nose, "I'll see you later"). Compelled to find my someone, I coquettishly meandered to the Dairy Bar, and I found who I thought was my person, my (only ever platonically considered [previously]) friend, A. He kept me safe as I danced in and out of sane behavior, taking off my shoes and shoelaces and throwing defiantly my sweatshirt, glasses, and cell phone out of my moving passenger's seat and demanding he feed me a ham sandwich despite my thirteen-years-old vegetarian status and attempts to climb into the university sheep pastures and attempts to make the final human baby with and watched him cry a little as I told him he was Fred Rogers and Adam and better than anyone ever and laughed a little when I said he looked like Ness from NES and called him a patient one who could take all the time he wanted and listened to people screaming in the ER with and listened to as he corrected me when I said they were bad actors to make those kinds of cries and interrupted him in the bathroom at my apartment (out of the sudden sinking fear he was going to try to kill himself in there [because he looked like Luke Wilson's character in *The Royal Tennenbaums* and my new bathroom looks like that bathroom]) and saying in what coded language I could manage that I (loved him and) (found him and) needed his help to get my (IUD out if we were going to make the last baby on earth, the one that will save humanity after this present apocalypse) missed dose of (daily; essential) medication. He took me to the hospital instead.

It was fun there (because I could watch people trying to get their kids to sit still and watch HGTV, and when the nurse asked me if I had any allergies, I told her my secret about amoxicillin, shitting my pants in my sleep, and hiding the evidence when I was a little kid), then it was cold (and I hid inside of a wadded cloud in the dark), and then it was scary (because I thought the angry bumps and bangs of people conducting construction in the hospital were the storming, uncontrollable emotions of my dad when he was angry at me as a child), and then I fell asleep wondering, "When's Father's Day?"

THE FLEX ROOM

I remember waking up knowing I was not home.

I remember discovering there was a one-way window in my room I hadn't
noticed the day prior.

I remember there were no other windows.

I remember knowing I was not myself when I was put in this space.

I remember suddenly remembering I let a horse out during and shakily
telling the social worker.

I remember worrying I had hurt my neighbor.

I remember trying to locate the biological inspiration to my touching the sun.

I remember thinking it might be black mold but not being able to say it
might be black mold.

I remember the social worker saying to someone "We have no idea what's
in the pot around town."

I remember laughing at seeing "safe" written on my food and a nurse
disregarding my notice.

I remember spontaneous confusion when a psychiatrist tried to help me
name why I was here.

I remember not being able to name why the meanies made me scared and sad.

I remember the exasperated look the social worker gave the psychiatrist
at my state.

I remember the psychiatrist saying as he left, "She's the boss!"

I remember my friend saying, "I could tell something was up."

I remember how the faces in the room looked down as I said
    'transnational missile' to a trans nurse.

I remember my other friend telling me it was Father's Day.

I remember weepily saying "I fell down" when my mother arrived.

I remember waking up in the night to her quietly crying by my bed.

I remember another nurse whispering to me, "Did you try to
    kill yourself?"

I remember a loved one asking me if I was trying to kill myself.

I remember knowing I was in trouble but not what kind.

I woke up several times during my stay through the bursting of receding manic bubbles boiling within me.

Something of the former day's psychosis stuck to me for the week I was on unit. By this, I mean I was still between realities for the first half of my stay, cognizant of something being amiss but walking through pairs of slanted hallways in that cognizance, making me rely upon the unstated trust that this place wasn't threatening my life and mind despite all the work Ken Kesey did to warp irreparably the public image of safe places for the highly confused to glean orientation.

One moment of alertness I experienced entails a loved one.

I was being transferred from The Flex Room. I was directed into a single occupant room with a bed and a window, and I was putting away a paper bag with my original outfit; my street clothes were replaced at intake with a blue paper shirt and pair of pants and medicinal gripper socks. It was then my loved one sat down on the edge of my bed, quietly stepped into a vocal register I had identified as protective but in need of answers, and said to me, "If this is an attempt at trying to kill yourself, you need to tell me now." My breath immediately became tight and I felt the pinpricks of sudden tears: Was I trying to kill myself? I didn't know, but I swore up and down that I didn't think so. I really was just trying to figure out what was going to happen next in my reincarnating adventure. Waves were still rippling out of me in my plea. My loved one said, "Okay." They've since apologized, but I don't think that was needed. We were both reaching out to catch the other in the same moment, having not realized we weren't falling anymore in gesturing. I was scared but only as a toddler is when looking to a taller person for direction on how to feel having fallen down and not known how to react; that's a survivable kind of fear and one that has no place for registering shame or guilt, just looking in the direction of the recognized and trustable for feedback on the situation neither of us was clear on. I'm a fortunate fuck to have this loved one in my life as they are. So fortunate.

Another moment of alertness comes from the second night I was on the unit.

Upon entry to the unit, beyond having my clothes returned, and a notebook and pencil and toiletries given to me, I was given a question-and-answer packet. I knew what it was at some level having majored in general psychology in undergrad: an index measuring something about my person. It was a thick packet, something like four hundred questions with either Yes/No or multiple choice answers. I was told to fill it out as soon as I could so the doctors could read the findings. It felt familiar in that I knew how to follow directions and had the awareness of a grade school child: catching phrases between quasi-watching adults; noticing street clothes differentiated the residents from the medical staff, who wore scrubs, professional wear, or lab coats; catching a bulletin from the police who were looking for a woman who was reported missing after having knocked on several neighbors' doors earlier that morning playing from a radio tuned to a local station; noticing that almost everybody in the place was white save for a lone woman of color who was fascinated with my presence, making me nervous but unsure why; an older woman on the unit who, while friendly, constantly gave advice and tried to make others around her feel better having listened to her. I wanted to do my homework, something I knew how to do and that's brought me out of my points of confusion before, so I tried, reading thoroughly and screwing in place my answers with my pencil, beyond simply focused. But the older woman came over to me on my couch and began talking to me. She told me of her life, how she had a dog boarding business that she built from the ground up. The dogs were pampered and coifed and given treatment usually reserved to humans like whole rooms to themselves or raised mattresses and matching handmade blankets. The whole shebang! But then she came here, and as soon as she filled in her test and handed it in, her whole life was ruined. She claimed to be $100,000+ in debt, because she was stuck in here, losing business and total control of her life's work thus far. So, don't finish that thing. Just lose it somewhere in here and tell them you can't find it. I thanked her for the insight, because holy shit, where am I? Then again, she wasn't a source of recognized authority, (e.g. She wasn't in scrubs, and the people in scrubs seem to be like teachers, my folks, and they wouldn't give me this index to lose it. I want answers, but I also know that if I stay here for a while, that'll be okay. I don't want to be on an adventure now. I want to do my homework.). So, I did my homework with a skip of extra haste and turned it in. She saw me and I saw her seeing me hand it in. She walked away, looking puzzled and deep in thought on figuring something out she couldn't name either. Shortly after, I tried to go to bed, but I didn't feel safe closing my eyes with her coming in and out of the bedroom we shared, looking at me in bed, and then walking back out muttering to herself, knowing she was scaring me but too nervous to leave me alone. (I know. It's okay. I promise. Just hang in there with me.) I went to the nurse's station after about four rounds of her checking on me, letting them know I was scared and didn't know what to do. They took me to a separate room, one that had one of those blue tumbling pads on the floor you'd find in a kindergarten Phys Ed room. I felt compelled to start explaining the current situation from the start of my psychosis, and the nurse who'd escorted me to the room eventually had to interrupt me and walk away since I was only escalating to sleepy tears in my not being able to communicate my confusion with this witness. I wanted help in my confusion, and I just didn't seem to know how to get that point across on satisfying terms yet. I eventually went back to my bed, and the older woman had disappeared.

At some point in my stay when I'd stopped counting days, I was invited to join in a yoga session with a visiting teacher. The young woman who was instantly drawn to me decided to come along, too.

This young woman revealed she was an undergrad at the same institution where I was going for my graduate degree, but she would not tell me her first name. Instead, she directly stated, "You can call me 'L.'" I wondered how many other letters she'd gone by since taking up the directive practice. I also appreciated that sense of asserting agency ahead of herself for herself. Like telling someone your pronouns prior to being asked just so that's crystalline and providing of structure in referral. I could understand, too, how there may be a need to maintain that kind of privacy while here and existing as the solo person of color. What has the world provided that would suggest trustworthiness in such a place? She even told me while I was experiencing some trepidation about my sanity that "Oh, yeah. This place is prison." I suddenly remembered my next-door neighbor's six-year-old daughter looking into my apartment window and calling to me through the window screen to play with her despite me being in bed and still a bit of a stranger. "I hope I didn't hurt that little girl," I said. "You better not have!" my peer said. I shut myself into that fear, trying to place the memory along the timeline of The Day, coming up nil having been alone in my apartment at the time in the girl memory but never during The Day memories. And at one point as I was speaking with a recreation leader, the leader stated, "It smells like vinegar. Do you smell that, too?" I did, and I knew exactly why we were smelling it. The young woman earlier had requested oil and vinegar from the mess, because she was dissatisfied with the toiletries she was given at the moment of her intake. They weren't gentle on her hair type. I could hear she was showering and washing her hair with the surreptitiously acquired vinegar as a gentle rinse and might have planned to run a bit of the oil through her hair after her shower to retain moisture better. I'd done it many times in the past to save a dollar and go for a gentler cleanse on my hair, and I recognized the pattern. But I suspect because it was a furtive move on her part, she was viewed as doing something that may be responded to punitively by the staff. I said nothing, and the rec leader went in search of the smell's source. I regret not saying anything.

However private the young woman was with some outward aspects of her identity, she often kept notes of our conversations as they were happening without attempting for privacy in the notetaking. I saw them once by accident; they didn't seem to make sense to anyone but her, as she was entirely devoted to keeping records for later examination. I was doing the same thing in my own way, but I had the fortune of some chemical clarification happening that had brought my two realities into better focus, and even then, I was rejoining our socially agreed upon reality without effort. I could tell she was still in her body's ethers, and she left her seat by me in a daze but staring directly into my eyes. She needed to float away, and I wasn't about to stop her. She deserved her holy, precious effort uninterrupted, and I wasn't going to be of service to her in my own fragilities. But I hoped she would draw closer to our shared reality soon. I could really use someone to talk to who'd touched the light, too.

This is not to say I wanted to use her. It's to state that we were both adrift, but I had a finishing current pushing me away from her, and that didn't feel fair to her from my view. She was working so much harder, and all I had done was watch the water in order to get back ashore.

Back to the yoga moment.

We were directed to the carpeted common room area where extra plush public chairs were arranged in a squarish, séance shape facing one another. The young woman grabbed a slightly thicker yoga mat and opened it to my left. I said something about the brain-cooling effects of yoga, how it was like I had, as a dear friend had put it once to me, a moment to "babysit" my brain. "Was that shade?" she asked in lighthearted inquiry, thinking my comment a joke. "No, that's what I really mean. Like it's a chance to step in and out of your own line of focus." The young woman looked at me with wider eyes, barely shook her head in a 'no', and swept away just as the yoga teacher started calling out poses and movements.

I say these things not to frighten anyone. These moments come back to me sometimes, pouring my morning coffee, taking a shower, rising through the steam, and they remind me how to distinguish where worlds meet and how they meld when caught in fog.

I need to backtrack a little bit.

Once I was delivered inside the hospital, still in active psychosis, I recall the specific rooms it took for me to reach an unusual place, one I wasn't predicting for intake into what I had partially recognized was a helping place along my journey.

My finder-friend kept me company in nearly all of them. (This person was and is a good, good person.)

The first room was the Emergency Room's waiting space. I briefly marveled at the God-like tableau vivants shown on the screen. The sight was breathtakingly expected as I read the messages that the shows were sending (but poorly hiding) subconsciously to viewers. I felt privy to an insight that had yet to be discovered, like being first in on some enormous authority's strategy for domination but only inside your head, like being at the front of an insurrection of a nation's Capitol building and laughing uncontrollably for how easy it is to break in without being stopped. Remembering how I wanted to ride a bicycle through a museum one day for the sake of breaking with propriety and experiencing living, unfettered joy in doing so, I tried to do a cartwheel to the bathroom adjacent to the waiting space. I failed but didn't fall, hearing my name being called by the front desk. I saw no reason to resist, sat down with the intake nurse (pre-Covid times), and without interest in shame, answered every question to the best of my abilities and with a gleeful rapport. I was happy and I felt like that example could bring levity to an already splendid day, bringing others in tow.

I am not wholly certain which came first, my private emergency holding room or my MRI, but I don't remember actually being still in a tube with a red light ahead of me. I know that it happened because an MRI is needed for a psychotic diagnosis, but there's seriously nah dah up there for me, and in that way, I occupy a more common space for those who experience psychosis. Most people don't remember it. I'm lucky?

After what I assume was my MRI, I was handed disposable paper clothes, socks, and a pee cup. I recall handing the pee cup to the nurse attending me as if I were about to receive the Eucharist for my acquiescence of a task. However, I forgot to put the cap on the container before I offered it up to this stunning but oddly busy goddess; she grabbed it with two fingers, flushed the toilet behind me with her sneaker, and ushered me to my private room. As we walked, smile burning bright on my face, I saw another nurse and winked at him as if to say, "Just you wait for my next trick."

My finder-friend joined me in the private holding room. He wore a ball cap, a backpack, and shorts with functional pockets, and because his out-fit was composed of mostly primary colors, I thought he was Ness from what little I knew of him in Nintendo games. I laid on the gurney-ish, beddish thing in the center of the room, trying to entice my finder-friend to come over and join me in a romantic embrace. He wouldn't budge, and I assumed that was because he was shy, and I said, "No rush. You take your time when you're ready. I'm in no hurry." After all, who knows where The Fury Road ends. Then, I wanted to sleep, bliss drunk. But I persevered in keeping my eyes open just long enough for a nurse to come in and take a blood sample. Because I had said, "Panic at Needle Park" several times in succession to my finder-friend, I remember he said with a jokish heart, "Well, I know she doesn't like needles." I didn't know what made that funny then. I just saw the connection and let it lie.

What I was really trying to say to my finder-friend during my "Needle Park" moment was, "Joan Didion. Joan Didion had this kind of adventure. I wonder if I'm the next Joan Didion." Forgive: I just wanted to dream of better than the last living situation I was in and to have that better achieved by my own means.

Really, I should have recognized I was potentially psychiatrically encumbered by my readership over the three prior years.

For the classes I taught, I selected texts that were written by and featuring women experiencing Bipolar I and II, specifically "The Special Special Special" by Maria Bamford and *Marbles* by Ellen Forney. I had themed my composition teaching material around coping and personal agency in moments of vulnerability. Essentially, I wanted to offer survival guides from as wide a series of authors as possible to invite the students into the texts from their own perspectives rather than simply white, heteronormative, and readerly-capitalizing examples. I wanted them to see they, too, were possibly humans and might be able to embrace certain elements of identity if provided living, breathing universally feminist success stories. I secretly wanted my students to not make the same freshman mistakes I did, like my eating disorder, my inherited whiteness, and independent errors in judgement due to pretty much any unconscious, unidentified inequity. I lost sight of the fact that this was a composition class I was teaching, and not all academic writing pursues data from a contextualizing intention. Sometimes, it's just about measuring the number of blinks a person makes to see how many they make in a given moment. Larger conclusions aren't always accessible to all. That's where I pushed back most in my teaching, the purposeful public-inaccessibility intention. I wanted education to be gathered from the gatherer's language and starting factors, not the greater institution (e.g. Academia)'s present status quo. Yes, rise to the occasions if you can and will, but hold on to that starting goal of wanting to understand from your own awareness and means of the world. If it does not serve you as a collectively-minded, connected thinker and maker, you should be allowed to enter and exit phases of intrigue on your own schedules and at your own economic place without diminishment of materials' accessibility. Or so I built my classes around at some level. What I wasn't aware of was just how much I wasn't acknowledging in my readership and points of identity. "Why do I understand what it feels like to be on fire for hours on end, having forgotten how to eat this last day, week, month? How come I'm not frightened enough of getting ill from the rats in my apartment not being addressed for months, and instead so aware of and familiar with the struggles to make sense of behaviors these writers and public figures were doing? Why did it take one of the people who moved me out of that living situation saying, "We didn't know when you were going to get sick," for me to realize I was actually already sick and in mortal danger? Why do we get comfortable within the acuity of vision that occurs sometimes in witnessing a tornado's tearing through your house? Is it a failure of my sympathetic system to recognize a need to flee at consciously recognized serious event, or is it my instinct to wait for certain guidance, for that insight that says, "You've been here before. Tread as you know how and with no turn of the head from the new eyes before you. There's something important to learn here."

Someone was screaming very near the private holding room. The someone was male in sex organs and wholly removed from the grace of their own mediation, wailing like a broken bone, a purely affecting vocalization of something skeletal in pain. But I was on an adventure, you see. There was no pain where I was, only representations of the thing, so this he-some agonist was clearly a red herring. Just laugh in marvel at the craftsmanship of the makeup on his face and wade the ear piercing until it's cried out. My finder-friend corrected my error, saying, "Oh, no. That's very... real." I did not think about what that meant.

DAY 44

Settle down if you can be
still at the mouth
and let water, let bread

Take to furling upon sills
while counting rice and radio
stations tucked behind knees

Coffee rings of theory,
the pantry of chapped hands
by bottled, burnishing wind

Were there another way to see
you than rounded by sticking
pixels, beads suggesting face

Of course, this is forever.

This, the press of petals between
fingers, the popping rhyme
of flame and flesh

Vesper dangs at noon
but birds
wound to branches like letters

May your god in mint ropes visit
for only a week, how ever those are
counted, by sand or stair

Through glass, paper, or shock
a wave passes
until onto the next

But then I watched a movie, and I felt better
because all the women were at different stages of being different
women, and with it being my birth
-day, I needed to feel like I wasn't only
stuck in my body
so much my body I have
to do something about the way I
applaud the fluffy roots slivering the peat
plugs in my aquaponic system even though there aren't
any fish yet
aggregating my plans for an inside roving orchard
and if there are going to be babies, Baby, Judy Blume is going to be in the house,
too, yielding answers
so as to suggest there's more than one
to any question you may have,
but all I need is one and that's too much to properly hold
an infant, mind its head, the hearth,
heaped with fancy
unlit candles and plastic juniper for Jesus, and for some
reason, my mother
thought it wise to let me do the decorating then
maybe to catch up for my happening two days after
Thanksgiving, her little feasty beasty who couldn't
figure out food so, instead, fell in love with the dishes
it came in, because it always would, this time
it took with two-story flames, and so she gave
buckets back but without the slack
of any other witness until the fires were quelled—proof
of the ability to withstand three straight hours of being
not at all sure she wasn't going to die there
on the rural island with the man and the dog and nothing else

appeared to her as problematic, another word in need of replacing,
like all the faucets in the house, I ran, spitting from each joint
water, sopping the counters in an ex post facto uh-oh let's go
call the fire department—No
way out there, alone, and the man said no give me a fucking bucket
and he was proud when he visited with me
the charred hayrack still hooked to his truck,
the two steel barrels burned through,
the halo of what were weeds six feet from a dried bean field
where he started it
the Saturday prior
to a brotherly surprise Sunday phone call
without a "What's up, Big Sister?" starter
gun shot to a race
I've always known I'd have to run some day.

It's been a month.

I have a new fish and fig
tree next to it.

I even refinished an end
table that was in one of the barns.

My partner came with me.

They came with me here to the burnt farm

and I don't know what to do

but write another list.

Autumn Toad

A frost came as it would any other: not too early,
not too late to count as the beginning or the end of any
one season. That feeling of death when in loose dirt,
wondering if you'd make it out from a slide before your
notice of breath. He had an auger in his left hand's electric
drill, his right hand pressed full weight into the right thigh
in order to stand, balancing on the head of the loose screw:
he reached the end of the battery's life, seventy-five holes
later, needing to catch his breath; his "mixtape" about to turn
over, The Man wanted to plant bulbs about the yard for Spring.
That's all, really.
He wanted a pond of lilies about the clover and allium ringing around the oaks.
And an entire bed of daffodils! So what that it's taken
how many bulbs s'is it taken? How many
have we done? And where did we start? Okay
so, just, maybe, a little, over, here, then? (I'd let him leave on his own accord right
about here. He's just between his last chord and his hand; let him rest.)
Then, I'd place a specific flat stone atop the darker, damp clayed soil
to mark the last hole I'd filled once I started the process again next.
In the morning, I'd found a toad ass up, asleep in the hole.
I turned his stony body so I could fit, too, a bulb
and covered the two, not caring who'd grow back out first.

Ephemeral Tattoos

A murmuration of startlings, a marrow disturbed:
the glassblower knew this could happen ahead of us,
her iron pincers coaxing fortune from the hallowed ball.

I swerved at the ready while attempting to unboil an egg in me, in-
stead slithering
the whole glistering yolk from my mouth
to yours to mine again, eyes closed and hissing.

A yew, mourning in the noonday, approached with temperance,
dropped her dress, and burst into a dust story, tinkling
with each former ring's intelligent witness.

What will it take—truly—what will it take
to hold still long enough to capture the man in his own wailing
child,
wailing back at it for wailing's sake?

And after all that, a hillock of uninterruptable bluebells.
Hush a bye. Hush a bye.
Hush a bye.

THE FAILURE'S INHERITANCE

Calumnies of colonies of then and now are not allowed
the privilege to bow upon their exits, and I'm recalling the weight of two
painted pewter bookends stowed in my father's office.
One in grey and the other blue, the two held in place
a collection of mourned Antebellums and Lincoln tributes, all looking
          anywhere but
the reason for the war for the reason for the war.
On their grassish pedestals, they stand in that same dare
to remember specifically who was considered a who,
placed just so by my father's engine-shamed hands.
How right the room is at the core of the house, his diecast
statutes at the ready beneath decades of yield reports, loan documents,
          unopened bills.
How right a house burns to six hundred degrees and pewter melts at four.

Imagining the Heat Death of the Universe While Holding My First-Born Nibling

Hildegard of Bingen once depicted genesis as a diamond in the sky
containing souls to be born. A comet's tail guides
the soul into the belly of a woman lying like a drape
of creeping rosemary in an oval vignette. Is it possible
to relay well enough the coming wounding of living,
to hold together another's trials still and clear before them
within their early days like a mosquito full
of prehistoric blood waiting in amber, piqued for both
flight and fury? Ducklings are sometimes born
in owl holes, forcing them upon hatching to drop
eighteen feet to the forest floor like a base jumper
without a parachute. But you don't need
metaphor to see the animal that you are. Afterall,
you can hold yourself up, clinging by a sapien
instinct inside your miniscule yet fully formed hands. But Dante
got it right, I think, so know that if you hold
your legs to your chest while fallen
in an iced lake, you'll keep warm. Know, too,
it's okay to call for rescue.

Meaning comrade
in arms, meaning
My incantations come
true: madder matters have
busied the pestle
enough. Scraping the fine
hair between her lips and teeth,
she wades the crowd again,
suckling upon the brush
for the velvet
of nouveau quaternity.
An ultramarine dune
at the ready, thick with visions,
dictations. For once, purple is the lesser,
a common offering: a hopeful staircase.
And from the mouth,
babes; a tip of the tongue
and she-spells: the making's meal; flecking
her belly and throat forever
in lapis lazuli, her teeth
like sandbars in the sky.

Strawberry grass.
The air lumbered in the light and loosened in the night.

A caul does not shed on its own; it takes a grasping, a catch
upon the whey of blood and bedding. I rose with dawning knees having
landed

from weird height with a whetting gasp. Mother needed
a week before trusting me to sleep in the reeds on my own,

as if my spots would fail. But when the universe falls from your belly,
you tend not to believe you'll catch it before some bottom does.

Rather than complain, I ate myself into body, cutting quick top teeth,
to prove it could hold. I tucked away the wonderment ribbons

I'd collected between her arrivals, knowing it wasn't time for glamor any-
more.
She thought me something beauty troubled enough: why invite misdirec-
tion?

We collected bachelor's buttons, milkweed, and dogbane blossoms to set
order:
the world grows with intentions, some of them to flirt

with the deeper goal to stop, so look but don't touch. So, I fell in love
with green from shadow, let its needles, not its lilacs, be my bed.

This is not to say I lied; I waited, a happy child with piqued bell ears,
took the fruited breath I was granted. Nothing more.

THE REDEEMER

Simply I daisy
and gallop the wending
tapestry for God. For me,
I taste a cinnabar frame
of mind, the young and old
fibers so marveled
for their possibilities, their lies
in comparison to what was
divined. Were it not dream,
would I be heard closer,
believed less loosely?
I waver the Earth, its concentricity
plain upon the map:
one, two, and three. The sky
needs no pupils to see the fields
woven below, the swirl of the breast
of the scent-loving fawn
bent to poppies white as caul,
and the lithe dace looking
askance at the love of gulls.
Here is your egg tooth, dear griffin.
Your angel's run a'ground.

Asylum

The dependence of hunger gives
way to a sharpened eye, a test subject
unsure if it's in the control or the experiment
group. Sugar or water or the choice to leave
before someone else's decision: paint me
a reverie like a radio dial or a waiting room's
splintering pique for your name. I want you
to take my time. When a succulent is
overwatered, it melts from the bottom up,
irretrievable from a surplus, watching itself
drown on land. I snake a string of pearls
around the pot to give it something of the sea
to welcome it while wasting; a terminal
lucidity in its shrinking. And you take my time kindly by
the spoonful, certain to slip the knife
from my teeth, and how I love you harder for it.
When you're not looking, I lick the counters:
Stray coffee grounds, mistaken yogurt dabs, cracker dust,
anything to keep the taste of you in my mouth even while
you're here. We're here. For now,
we draw a bath to forget that
RBG is dead, and what was scalding, we let turn cold
to know we're still warm inside. What endurance
do we need to carve from ourselves next?
I'd carry your child if you'd have me, provided I still can
or ever could in these days of petroleum skin on the lake
shivering beneath wildfire smoke and Baldwin
rightfully back in vogue. Would one be a fortune? Salt!
Salt for the going, for the polish of the pearls.
Where next the dishes and chairs are placed matters
as much as the light and the will to eat.

THANKSGIVING

A cuttlefish named Preservation is at the dining table, wicking patina
off a silver butter plate with a turquoise rag in one tentacle
and adjusting with another the linen runner in order to hide
the more obstinate wine splatters. A candlestick the shape of an ear
of shucked corn rolls away from its parallel mate, knocked to
motion by an ireful stacking of eight months' copies of The Economist
by a six foot, actively fraying rubber band ball. A wadded canvas
dropcloth gets kicked for being in the ball's way, flecks of toffee and mulch
shaking out like dandruff on the parquet. Not finished yet,
the unpatterned registries of childhood bedrooms occupying
plastic tubs around the floor get shoved and lambasted until Preservation
sweeps them out of the ball's path, stretching a third, fourth, and fifth
tentacle to the task. Fair ribbons hung in maypole fashion around
                                            swimming trophies,
school play posters slithering beneath diary attempts, photos of people
who've shuffled out of their names: the open tubs are salvaged into a fort
around the busy fish, saved for assessment by forthcoming reroosters.
The ball rumbles off in search of a book on Yellowstone, sees the dog
wants back in, acquiesces the pied brindle pupper, and gives in to a bouncy
tussle. The oven timer beeps in alarm like a dump truck in reverse: pie
number two is done. But the ball doesn't know this, and Preservation
explains the sound to cool the upset, trying to balance the next three
dishes needing baking. A Pyrex dish—oyster casserole--skids from the
                                            cephalopod,
the grip on her squishy dome just not enough for the rate of movement.
Clatter platter, but thankfully, the ball decided to vacuum, masking
the noise. The cuttlefish cleans up the mess, the dog and ball too focused
on their task to interrupt, which the fish tries not to resent since they can't
help it: they're a dog and ball; it's not in their nature. Tentacles seven
and eight are feeling sore, so Preservation pours a cup of coffee and rests
with it after setting the timer again. The ball comes into the kitchen,

grabs a mug, too, and chuckles *So, what we doing, just cruisin' for biscuits?* Bizarre but adorable, it's the kind of thing that brought Preservation here. So, it's laugh out a response and sip and titter into the cup and nosh on string cheese and leftover potato salad until the front door opens.

BIG BIRD IN CHINA

Her smiling head, tilted at a shy angle,
and the great span of steps and space-seen
stone winding into split green:

(Did cameras then always tint the world
a bettering blue? A prescient color
for storytelling?)

she looks so young.

--

Xiao Foo taught me the characters
for 'speak' and 'rain,' and as its tender
beard unwhorled, big brother juddered
about the butter and sugar iris
outside the kitchen bay window.

He's back! Big Bird's back!

Nǐ hǎo, Big Bird. You're in time for pizza.

--

Nixon not yet nixed and H.W. liaising
before a new decade, my mother

let her name flash diplomatic with forty-nine
other U.S. teachers and doctors in exchange
for first-hand time with the nouns
of the translated texts she mastered.

Five years later, Carol Spinney came, too.

Neither was prepared for the bicycles.

--

In the glass-faced cabinets are two bamboo
and silk fans. One is spread open.

At the door to the porch, a tiger
fires into the unpainted, fury-eyed.

I'll show you my slides one day.

--

She chased no monkey kings,
sought no headless water buffalo.

A gold bandana tied to her head
as she crossed Tiananmen and the Forbidden
City; solo treading and outward adjustments;
the pepper she hid hearing white housewives
complain about eating watermelon again.

--

When home sick, mom

taught me to watch Barkley romp
with his avian companion
over bridged pools and
chessboard mountains.

I can still paint 'rain.'

TULIPS AND THE LION BOY

for Lev, Jude, and Seth

Heavy headed, each slow to graze
new earth; waxed, meandering
napes edging over their glass:
walking canes made for marvel.

    Between their swoop—licks
    of the ruling crown

in full flame. With no stop to his trills,
love-drunk on the world, he peals
back layers of name
    Oye-ni! Eye-knee! Ay-nay!
while held to his throne.

Jubilantly indigo, silhouette rimmed
talc by the early afternoon bricks
behind, his topsy animal doesn't wait
for physics to approve decree.

Each impossible fingernail considered
by song; paints bubbled away,
the next wonder piece needs
finding. Instead, of course, he fills
in both ends of volley
    Big Rafi, the Giraffeey!
    Where is he? He's hidin'.
    There he is!

Vibrating cools in a gust, and
he pins to an unmoored
radio. In sways to coax streams,
those weedy limbs lengthen to
their softer extents.
By the doorknob's tongue:
                    prayers aloft

You're better than the baby in the barn.

TRIPTYCH

I'll call you a punk
if I wanna, and I wanna, so you're a punk, Punk. Listen, Popaloo, let's
ease up on the
expletive fire- bombing while problem- solving.
I know, I know. I find it hilarious,
personally, dropping
fucks like commas. Nobody does it like you. But apparently, it ain't ladylike,
        and those veins
of yours have had enough. That sounds
frustrating. The docs
don't know your baseline's a spicy curmudgeon. If you wanna head to the car,
I'll be right there. Just gotta ask the nurse about this medicine.

Want lunch? Now,
don't make me
put googly eyes on the contents of the fridge
again. It's harmless, but you gotta take them
off before snarf sessions, dude. Alarm clocks and boxed granolas are
       cabinet-safe, bub. Oh. Okay. I'll leave it. I'm sorry. Would it be
       alright if I
put the dish soap under the sink rather than in the bag of rock salt?
       Thanks
for cleaning the carpets! Must've been you. Sorry. I thought you were
       the only one who knows how to use the shampoo thingy. Okay.
Sorry 'bout that. My bad.

Tell me about the birds. Have the Redstarts come back this year? Aw. L'il pluckers. I heard MJ made friends with a skunk. Y'all were made
for
each other. Just gonna put your pills on the dresser. Well, where would you prefer them? Where are we gonna eat, then? Nevermind. No. It's okay. The road commissioner won't touch MJ. No,
I promise. He
won't come into the house. Hey.
Hey.

I got you.

The following pieces were previously published in:

My Animal of Then : GASHER Press
The Failure's Inheritance : The Paddock Review
Imagining... : Fatal Flaw Literary Magazine
Asylum : Electric Literature

ANNIE GOOLD is from a small farm in central Illinois. Her work has appeared in Matter, Electric Literature, The Paddock Review, GASHER, Fatal Flaw Literary Magazine, and elsewhere. She graduated with an MFA in Poetry from Cornell University in 2017. She lives and writes in Urbana, IL

www.ingramcontent.com/pod-product-compliance
Lightning Source LLC
Chambersburg PA
CBHW011218120626
46545CB00008B/3043